Focus on prevention

Embrace your individuality in a positive manner.

Strive for wellness.

Create harmony within yourself.

Know your strengths and make them stronger.

Eat healthy, exercise some, sleep sound.

Constantly do things that improve your health.

Expect unexpected blessings.

Clean daily.

Choose to see beauty even if things appear ugly.

Share knowledge.

To educate is to illuminate.

Read daily to give your mind exercise.

Read to succeed.

Learn to earn.

Knowledge pays biggest dividends.

Love self.

Show self love every day.

Love of self and others is important for health.

Get second opinions as many times as needed.

Focus on faith in faith.

You are your present. Live in it with gratitude.

Speak truth otherwise speak silence.

Think of the best.

Learn from everything and everyone.

Rest increases strength.

Positive attitude enhances healing and wellness.

Embrace healthy routines.

Good health care helps you feel your best.

Participate actively in your health care.

Teaching kids about health gives healthy attitudes

Keep your mind healthy.

Good food, good health.

Good health includes doing good things.

Keep a positive attitude.

Atonement strengthens mind, body, and spirit.

Forgive.

Following a healthy lifestyle is good self care.

Be good to yourself all the time.

Study and read for what you need for your health

Be literate in health.

Think good thoughts.

Meditate.

Eat right.

Exercise routinely.

Play.

Laugh.

Rest.

Pray.

Avoid stress and limit that which can induce it.

Breathe mindfully.

Get medical care before it is an emergency.

Be with those who support you in positive ways.

Thankfulness is healthy.

Express gratitude often.

Seek goodness.

Inspire compassion for good health and wellness.

Meditate to illuminate.

Laughter heals.

Anticipate the difficult by managing the easy.

Stay ready.

Be prepared for anything.

Refrain from wrongdoing.

Expect excellence.

Optimism opens.

Put your ideas into positive actions.

Compliment often.

Do work worthy of recognition in all you do.

Make charity a lifestyle.

Learn and grow at your own pace.

Value values.

Little changes make big differences.

Wisdom comes from experience.

Education enhances wisdom.

Change creates opportunities.

Opportunity is a gift.

Be open and receptive to your good.

Peace is conflict prevention.

Drink responsibly for drunkenness is unhealthy.

If it fails to the point of likely harm, leave it alone.

Be mindfully aware of being thankful.

Be happy despite uncontrollable unhappiness.

Daydream.

Read every day.

Listen more.

Cash may be king, but kindness is queen.

Do nice things daily.

Allow plenty of time to be on time.

Take your time instead of rushing yourself.

Exalt in good manners.

Loyalty is royalty.

Create passion.

Be kind to create more joy and happiness.

Keep learning.

Enjoy yourself.

Be fair in all you do.

Pray often.

Satisfy weakness with a dose of discipline.

Limit and avoid multitasking.

Ignore distractions.

Know your family health history.

Discontinue bad habits.

Focus forward.

If it fails to help you, let it be.

Connect to stillness daily.

You are a self healer.

Fill your life with those who love you.

Fill your life with those you love.

Appreciate gratitude.

Let go ego.

Good romance is healthy.

Think about your desire to be healthy and well.

Ask, believe, and receive.

Know your illnesses.

Use your imagination.

Act and speak in ways to encourage good health.

Be a good listener.

Tell the truth.

Give respect to everyone you encounter.

Educate yourself daily.

Read a lot.

Be compatible and compromising.

Honor your words with your actions.

Talk to those who listen.

Take a vacation at least twice a year.

Daydream more.

Enjoy each day planned or unplanned.

Make silence a routine part of your day.

Travel as much as you can.

Maintain for good gain.

Keep good thoughts in your mind.

Walk.

Keep your self esteem high.

Encourage yourself.

Keep good habits and make more of them.

Be a disciple of discipline.

Listen to yourself.

Live in the present moment.

Transcend to transform.

Save money.

Volunteer.

Each day is an opportunity to be your best.

Keep an open mind.

Love vividly, live long.

Good love, good health, good life.

Create true wealth with good health.

Keep your mind healthy.

Live in confidence.

Think.

Respect elders.

Expect success.

Love love.

Visualize positive outcomes.

Agree or disagree agreeably.

Sleep enough to keep well rested.

Make patience a virtue that comes naturally.

Take good advice.

Learn as much as you can.

Be a friend to those who need one.

Live in spite of illness.

Invoke patience infinitely.

Focus on doing better.

Make weak areas stronger.

Honor your worthiness.

Sacrifice builds strong spirit.

Be generous.

Give and receive.

Go to bed without anger.

Aging is an asset.

Enjoy several sports as a spectator.

Trust yourself.

Find funny and laugh daily.

Dance.

Look at nature inside and outside.

Encourage yourself.

Be a team player.

Know your health numbers.

Listen to other opinions.

Think calm to stay calm.

Prepare in prayer.

Do things that relax you.

Let anxiety be a thing of the past.

Keep a health diary.

Stay current.

Pursue many interests.

Unlimit yourself.

Be attentive to wisdom.

Find the knowledge of God.

Comfort others.

Respect your universal divinity.

Expect the best.

Let go of worry in a hurry.

Know yourself better than anyone else.

Let your mind unwind.

Purposeful planning prospers.

Own your actions and your words.

Write about yourself for yourself.

Cry when you need to.

Make your goals reasonable.

Walk upright.

Appreciate.

Make worry scurry.

Love yourself and love being yourself.

Be friends to those who keep confidences confident.

Give encouragement to others.

Eat beans and greens often.

Learn how to do all that makes you healthy.

Sing out loud.

Keep out doubt to keep your personal clout.

Real love is true love is real love.

Keep salt off the dining table.

Admire how beautiful you are.

Light the way to see where you are going.

Add an extra day to vacation.

Know when to step forward or back.

No pain is a big gain.

Appreciate.

Affirm faith.

Eat oatmeal for a daily pill.

Get a third opinion.

Keep copies of your medical record current.

Rest to get more zest.

Keep self doubt out for more self clout.

Cook often.

Be a money saver.

Maintain good hygiene daily.

Listen when someone else is talking.

Enjoy your own company.

Read aloud.

Smile more.

I am.

Affirm good before you get it.

Welcome change positively.

Get medical screening tests routinely.

Speak kindly of others.

Listen more than talk.

Make happiness the way every day.

Read more.

Keep good company.

Keep idle gossip idle.

Retire early.

Vacation staycation often.

Open doors for others.

Have many spiritual friends.

Refill prescriptions before they run out.

Fix the broken if you can.

Stretch your body and mind daily.

Know your diagnoses.

Avoid wasting anything.

Honor divinity.

Be trustworthy.

Be as happy as possible.

Listen to the rain.

Plant a garden.

Strive to make all you do better.

Respect.

Make lists for doctor appointments.

Share good fortune abundantly.

Communicate effectively.

Envision success in all you do.

Expect and accept good.

Give thanks.

Visualize healing and good health.

Eat lots of fruit and vegetables.

Walk every day.

Integrate health treatments.

See specialists for specifics.

Help those in need get up to speed.

Be attentive to your body's needs,

Go to bed and get out of bed early.

Wake up with a smile.

Go to sleep with a smile.

Give to charity.

Maintain as much self care as you can.

Natural healing is in you and around you.

Think positively of next outcomes as good.

Sleep enough.

Enjoy your family.

Manage your money to afford what you need.

Volunteer for worthy causes.

Prepare for all that you can see and forsee.

Think often of good memories.

Be patient with yourself and others.

Take time for quiet daily.

Close your day without anger.

Be unconditional love.

Thank YOU.

Made in United States
Orlando, FL
09 July 2023